Rosemary Hellyer-Jones

Snapdragon

D1735170

Ernst Klett Verlag

Stuttgart Düsseldorf Leipzig

Gedruckt auf Recyclingpapier,
hergestellt aus 100 % Altpapier.

1. Auflage   A 1 ⁴ ³ ² ¹ | 2001 2000 99 98

Zeichnungen: Elsie Lennox, London.
Druck: Wilhelm Röck, Weinsberg
Printed in Germany.
ISBN 3-12-570910-5

Contents

1. A dangerous animal*

There's a dangerous new animal in the garden, Susie. A frog!

A frog? No problem, Freddy. Toy frogs are OK.

But this frog isn't a toy, Susie. You wait!

Oh, Freddy! Do frogs like spiders?

Yes, they do! Hungry frogs ♥ spiders!

HELP !!!

animal ['ænɪməl]   Tier

4

2. All about frogs

Which answers are right*?

1. What colour are frogs? (Three answers are right!)
   green ☐   yellow ☐   black ☐
   brown ☐   red   ☐   white ☐

2. What do frogs do? (Two answers are right!)
   walk ☐   run ☐   jump ☐   swim ☐   roll ☐

3. What do frogs eat? (Two answers are right!)
   caterpillars ☐   popcorn ☐   spiders ☐
   grass*   ☐   apples ☐

4. What do frogs do in the winter? (One answer is right!)
   swim a lot ☐   look for food ☐   sleep ☐

5. How does a frog's life start? (One answer is right!)
   as* a baby frog ☐   as an egg ☐   as a caterpillar ☐

3. Mr Hop

"I can't find Mr Hop!"
"Mr Hop? Who is that?"
"My pet frog. He's lost."
"Don't worry! You can put
an ad in the newspaper*."
"That's no help. He can't read."

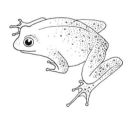

right	*hier:* richtig
grass [grɑːs]	Gras
as [æz]	als
put an ad in the newspaper [pʊt ən ˈæd]	eine Annonce in der Zeitung aufgeben

5

4. A rhyme: The bee*

"Buzz, buzz, buzz!" says the bee.
"These snapdragons are all for me!*
I can go from flower to flower,*
I can do it in an hour!
Buzz, buzz, buzz!" says the bee.

5. A day in the life of Biddy Bee: an interview

FREDDY: Here with me today is Biddy Bee.

BIDDY: Hi, Freddy.

FREDDY: Well, Biddy, what about a bee's day?

BIDDY: We have a very long day, Freddy! We work long hours, you see. Especially* in the summer months.

FREDDY: What do you have for breakfast, Biddy?

BIDDY: Honey*, of course! We have honey for lunch, too.

FREDDY: And where does the honey come from?

BIDDY: A lot of it comes from flowers. But it sometimes comes from trees, too.

FREDDY: How long are you outside in the summer?

BIDDY: We often work eight to ten hours. Sometimes twelve. Then we must work in the nest*, too.

FREDDY: Wow!

bee [biː]	Biene
snapdragon ['snæpdrægən]	Löwenmäulchen
flower ['flaʊə]	Blume
especially [ɪ'speʃəlɪ]	besonders
honey ['hʌnɪ]	Honig
nest	Nest

6

6. Always hungry!

Hi, Susie!

Oh, it's you, Freddy. Hey, are you having lunch? But it's only* eleven o'clock in the morning!

I know. But I'm hungry!

Hungry? You know something, Freddy? You're ALWAYS hungry!

only ['əʊnlɪ]   nur, erst

7. Ideas with ice cream – for hungry people

Peach* boat

Put* a half* peach on a plate*. Then put ice cream on it. Put a piece* of apple in the ice cream. Two or three jelly babies can 'sit' in the boat, too!

Banana split

Put two big 'balls' of different ice cream on a plate. (White ice cream and chocolate ice cream are good.) Then two long pieces of banana next to the ice cream. A banana split is nice with cream*, too!

peach [pi:tʃ]	Pfirsich
put	legen, setzen
half [hɑːf]	halb
plate [pleɪt]	Teller
piece [piːs]	Stück
cream [kriːm]	Sahne

8. The burglar

1. It's Saturday evening. Half past six. Carol, Kevin and Lester are at Linda's house. Linda's mother isn't at home. The friends are sitting in the living-room. They're watching TV.

5   "This film is boring!" says Kevin. He looks out of the window. There's a big house opposite Linda's house. "Who lives in that house over there, Linda?" Kevin asks.

"Mrs Green," Linda says. "She's new here. But she's in France now. She's on holiday."

10   "On holiday?" Kevin says. "But there's a light on in the house … And look, there's a car …"

"Maybe she's back from holiday," says Carol.

"No, she isn't," Linda says. "She's in France for two weeks."

15   "Who *is* in the house then?" Lester says.

"Maybe it's a burglar!" Carol says.

"We must phone the police!" Lester says.

"Yes, let's do that," says Kevin. "Where's the telephone, Linda?"

20 2. Now Linda is talking to a policeman on the telephone. "Yes, there's a light on in the house … Yes, it's number 23 Park Road … No, Mrs Green is away on holiday …"

"OK, we're coming," the policeman says. "Wait there."

3. The children are in the road now.

25   "That red car!" says Carol. "Maybe it's the burglar's car."

	burglar ['bɜːglə]	Einbrecher
12	**maybe** ['meɪbiː]	vielleicht
17	**phone**	telefonieren

"Let's take the number," says Linda. "Have you got a pencil, Kevin?"

"I have," says Lester. "Here you are, Linda."

"Hey, look! A police car! It's coming round the corner," says Kevin. "That's quick!"

The police car stops. There are two policemen in it.

"Is this the house?" asks the first policeman.

"Yes, it is," says Linda. "Look, the light is on in that window. And we think this is the burglar's car."

"OK, you can wait here," says the other policeman. "Don't come into the house with us. Burglars are sometimes dangerous."

4. The door is open, so the two policemen can walk into the house. The children are waiting outside. Now they can hear voices. From the house!

"What's going on?" It is a woman's voice. "The police? But what are you doing here?"

"That's our question! What are you doing here in this house?"

"You can see that!" says the woman's voice. "Look, I'm – "

"Hey!" says Linda suddenly. "That's Grandma's voice! Let's go in!"

5. Now they are all in Mrs Green's living-room.

"Grandma!" Linda says. "What are you doing here?"

"I'm feeding the fish," says Grandma. "Can't you see that?"

10	**other** [ˈʌðə]	andere, -r, -s
13	**so** [səʊ]	*hier:* also
15	**voice** [vɔɪs]	Stimme
25	**to feed** [fiːd]	füttern
25	**fish**	Fisch, Fische

There's a big aquarium in the room. There are a lot of fish in it. A lot of different colours. Yellow, red, green, blue …

"My friend, Mrs Green, is away for two weeks, you see, so I'm feeding her fish."

5 "Then there isn't a burglar here?" says Lester. "But what about the car outside?"

"The red car? That's my car," says Grandma.

"But you haven't got a red car, Grandma," says Linda. "Your car is green!"

10 "Not now!" says Grandma. "I've got a new car now – and it's red!"

"Oh no!" says Kevin.

"Well, we must go now," says the first policeman. "There are no burglars here – that's good."

15 "Sorry!" says Lester. "We – "

"That's OK. No problem!" says the other policeman. "Good night, all!"

6. "Mrs Green's fish are always hungry," says Grandma. "Are you hungry, too? Let's go to the new snack bar in 20 Long Street. They've got good hamburgers there, I think. Do you all like hamburgers?"

"Yes, we do! Great!"

"Thanks, Grandma!"

"OK then. Where's Mrs Green's key? Oh, here it is. 25 We can go."

Grandma closes the door and they all go to her new car. "Is there room for you all? – OK, let's go!"

1 **aquarium** [ə'kweərɪəm]   Aquarium
27 **room** [rʊm]   *hier:* Platz

9. Hungry again!

Hi, Freddy!
Hungry again?

Of course I'm hungry!
Yum! Yum!

You know what, Freddy?
I've got a new name for you.

A new name?
What then?

Freddy Elephant!

Very funny.

10. All about elephants

Which answer is right?

1. Elephants must eat a lot – because they're so big!
   Every day they eat for 10 hours ☐
   12 hours ☐
   16 hours. ☐

2. Elephants are sometimes dangerous.
   Every day elephants kill* about* 100 people ☐
   about 250 people ☐
   about 500 people. ☐

3. Elephants drink a lot of water.
   Every day an elephant drinks 50 litres* ☐
   150 litres ☐
   200 litres. ☐

4. A young elephant lives with its mother for
   2 years ☐   5 years ☐   10 years. ☐

5. An elephant has got
   four knees* ☐   two knees ☐   no knees. ☐

kill [kɪl]	töten
about	ungefähr
litre ['liːtə]	Liter
knee [niː]	Knie

11. Elephant corner

– How do you know when there's an elephant in your cupboard?
– Easy! You can't close the door.

★ ★ ★ ★ ★ ★ ★

– What do you do when you find an elephant in your bed?
– No problem! Sleep in another bed.

★ ★ ★ ★ ★ ★ ★

– How do you know when there's an elephant in your bed?
– You can see the 'E' on his pyjamas*.

★ ★ ★ ★ ★ ★ ★

pyjamas [pə'dʒɑːməz]   Schlafanzug

12. Bobby Bird

1. It's a summer afternoon. Kevin and Lester are playing a computer game in Lester's room. It's very warm, so they've got the window open. Suddenly they hear something.

"Chirp! Chirp!"

5 "What's that?" says Lester.

"It's a bird," says Kevin.

"But we haven't got a bird," says Lester. "And there are no trees here."

"Chirp! Chirp!"

10 "There it is again!" says Kevin. "It *is* a bird. But where?" The boys stop their game. Lester goes to the window and looks out.

"Chirp!"

2. "Hey, Lester, look behind you!" says Kevin. "It's on the 15 floor. It's a budgie!"

"Hey, isn't it nice?" says Lester. "And it's a nice colour, too."

The budgie is blue. Now it's sitting on Lester's bookshelf.

"Let's close the window," says Kevin. "Then it can't fly 20 away."

Lester closes the window. "Isn't it funny?" he says. "A budgie here at Parkway Towers! But where is it from?"

"Chirp! Chirp!"

bird [bɜːd]	Vogel
2	**warm** [wɔːm]	warm
4	**chirp** [tʃɜːp]	Pieps!
15	**budgie** ['bʌdʒɪ]	Wellensittich
19	**fly** [flaɪ]	fliegen

"It's talking to us," says Kevin. "Hey, budgie, where are you from?"

"Chirp! Bobby Bird! Bobby Bird!"

"Hey, listen, Kevin! It can talk! Listen!" says Lester.

5   "Bobby Bird! Chirp! Bobby Bird!"

"What is it saying?" says Kevin. "I can't – "

"Bobby Bird! Chirp! Twenty-two Field Street, Leeds!"

"What? Twenty-two Field Street?" says Lester. "It's saying where it lives, Kevin!"

10   "Say it again, budgie!" says Kevin. "Twenty-two Field Street?"

"Field Street, Leeds! Chirp!"

"But there isn't a Field Street in Leeds," says Kevin.

"Yes, there is," says Lester. "I know where it is."

15   3. Now Lester's mother is at home.

"What? A budgie?" she says. "And it can talk?"

"Yes, it's great! It can say where it lives. Twenty-two Field Street!"

"Well, you must take it there. It must go home."

20   "Come here, little budgie!" says Lester. "You must go home."

16

The budgie is on the bookshelf again. Lester goes to the bookshelf. But then the budgie flies to his bed on the wardrobe! Kevin is there.

"Come here, budgie!" says Kevin.

5 But it flies away again. Now it's on the computer.

"Come here!" says Lester's mother.

But the little bird flies away again.

"It's no good," says Lester. "We can't catch it!"

4. "Maybe we can phone its owner," says Kevin. "We know
10 the address."

"Yes, but we don't know the name!" says Lester. "It's no good."

"Bobby Bird! Chirp! Bobby Bird!"

"What's it saying?" says Lester's mother. "Bobby Bird?"

15 "It's saying its name," says Kevin. "Bobby. Bobby Bird."

"Bird! Chirp! Bobby Bird!"

"Hey, I've got an idea," says Lester suddenly. "Maybe the owner's name is Bird. You know, Bird is a family name, too."

"Is it? I don't know," says Kevin. "Mr Bird? Mrs Bird?
20 Funny idea!"

"Well, let's look in the telephone book," says Lester.

The telephone book is in the living-room.

"B. There are a lot of names under B," says Lester. "Banks – Batts – Benson – Best – … Wait … Bird! Yes,
25 there are five or six Birds here."

"Look at the addresses," says Kevin.

8	**it's no good** [ɪts nəʊ ˈɡʊd]	es hat keinen Zweck
8	**catch** [kætʃ]	fangen
9	**owner** [ˈəʊnə]	Besitzer/-in
10	**address** [əˈdres]	Adresse

"Wait, I've got it!" says Lester. "Bird, W., 22 Field Street, Leeds. That's it! Great!

"What's the number?" asks Kevin.

5. Now Mr Bird is at Lester's flat. He is carrying Bobby's cage.

"Come here, Bobby!" he says. The little budgie flies to the old man. Then it goes into its cage, and Mr Bird closes the little door.

"Well, thank you!" he says to the two boys. "I'm so happy! Now I've got Bobby back again!"

"Bobby is great!" says Lester. "Do you talk to him a lot?"

"Oh yes! I always talk to him. My wife is dead now, so I'm alone a lot. Bobby is my best friend."

At the door, Mr Bird gives Lester five pounds. He gives Kevin five pounds, too.

"Hey, thank you, Mr Bird!" they say. "That's nice!"

"You're welcome," says Mr Bird. "Goodbye!"

£ £ £ £ £ £ £ £ £ £

What can the boys do with ten pounds?

They can …
- go to the cinema.
- buy a budgie.
- go to a snackbar.
- buy a CD / a video.
- go to the zoo.
- have a party with their friends.

What's the best idea? Say what you think.

5	**cage** [keɪdʒ]	Käfig
12	**wife** [waɪf]	Ehefrau
13	**alone** [əˈləʊn]	allein

13. What's the time?

14. Bill and Bob *(A sketch)*

Two men, Bill and Bob, are at a bus stop in a street in town – at night. There are houses in the street.

Bob:	Great evening, Bill! Great party!
Bill:	Yeah! – Hey, Bob, what's the time?
5 Bob:	I don't know. Twelve o'clock, maybe? Or one?
Bill:	Haven't you got a watch?
Bob:	No, I haven't, Bill. Haven't *you* got a watch?
Bill:	No. but I *must* know the time, Bob! I must catch the last bus.
10 Bob:	Well, I don't know. – Ask that man over there.

Another man is walking down the street now. Bill stops him.

Bill:	Excuse me! What's the time, please?
Man:	Sorry, I don't know. Good night! *(He walks away.)*
15	
Bill:	Good night.
Bob:	There's a clock at the bus station, Bill.
Bill:	That's a long walk from here.

Suddenly Bob has an idea.

20 Bob:	Hey, I've got an idea, Bill. Let's sing a song!
Bill:	A song??? I can't sing, Bob.
Bob:	Yes, you can, Bill. What song do you know?
Bill:	'Happy birthday'?

5	**maybe** ['meɪbi:]	vielleicht
6	**watch** [wɒtʃ]	Armbanduhr
8	**catch a bus** [kætʃ ə'bʌs]	einen Bus kriegen

20

BOB:	No, we can't sing that. Your birthday is in March – and my birthday is in May. – What about the Alphabet Song?
BILL:	I don't know that, Bob.
5 BOB:	'Rock around the clock'?
BILL:	Yes, I know that. But what – ? What's the idea?
BOB:	Wait and see! – OK. Here we go then, Bill. ONE – TWO – THREE:

Bob starts the song. He sings very loud. Then Bill sings
10 *with him. Very loud, too!*

BOB (AND BILL):	One, two, three o'clock,
	Four o'clock rock!
	Five, six, seven o'clock,
	Eight o'clock rock!
15	Nine, ten, eleven o'clock,
	Twelve o'clock rock!
	We're gonna –

Suddenly an upstairs window opens. A woman looks
out of the window. She is wearing a nightdress. She is
20 *very angry.*

WOMAN:	What's going on? Do you know what time it is? It's half past two in the morning!! *(She closes the window with a bang.)*
BOB:	Thanks, lady! – There you are, Bill. It's half past
25	two!

7	**wait and see!** [weɪt ən'siː]	wart' mal ab!
9	**loud** [laʊd]	laut
19	**nightdress** ['naɪtdres]	Nachthemd
20	**angry** ['æŋgrɪ]	zornig, wütend
22	**half past two** [hɑːf pɑːst 'tuː]	halb drei

15. Let's make a paper snapdragon!

1. Take a piece of paper (16 x 20 cm).

2. Fold it in half.

3. Fold it again.

4. Open the fold on one side. Then fold the corners on three sides.

5. Do the same on the other side.

6. Fold the paper in half again – so the corners come together.

7. Find the middle, and make a small cut.

8. Fold the snapdragon's mouth.

9. Make the eyes with a felt-tip, or a black pencil.

10. Open the mouth outwards. – Look, there's your snapdragon! "Snap!"

1	**piece of paper** [piːs əv'peɪpə]	Blatt Papier
2	**fold** [fəʊld] **(in half)**	falten (zusammenfalten)
4	**side** [saɪd]	Seite
8	**together** [tə'geðə]	zusammen
9	**cut** [kʌt]	Schnitt
10	**mouth** [maʊθ]	Mund
11	**eye** [aɪ]	Auge
12	**outwards** ['aʊtwədz]	nach außen

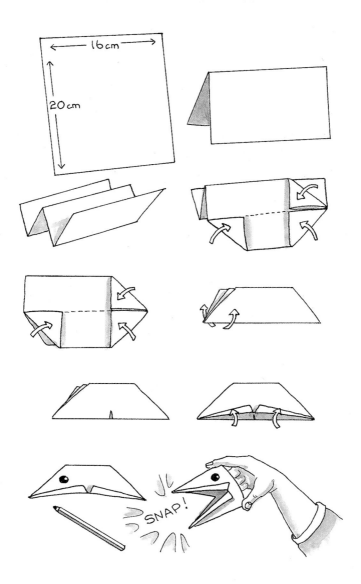

16. A walk – and an adventure

1. It is a Saturday afternoon in October. Carol, Linda and Lester are at Kevin's house. Whisky, the Parkers' dog, is with them in Kevin's room.

"Let's watch a video," says Lester.

5   "No, let's play a computer game," says Linda.

"We can't," says Kevin. "My brother is using the computer."

"Let's do something outside," says Carol. "I know what! We can take Whisky for a walk. Look, he wants to go out,

10 you can see!"

"Well, OK," says Kevin. "The weather is great for a walk. Come on, Whisky!"

Whisky runs to the door. He thinks a walk is a great idea.

15 2. "Let's go to the park," says Carol.

"No, we always go there," says Kevin. "Let's go to the ninety-nine steps. That's the best walk!"

"Yes, but it's a very long walk, Kevin," says Linda.

"The ninety-nine steps?" says Lester. "What's that?"

20   "It's a great walk. First you go through the woods. Then you go over the old railway line. There are fifty steps up.

1	**afternoon** [ɑːftə'nuːn]	Nachmittag
6	**use** [juːz]	benützen
12	**come on!** [kʌm'ɒn]	los!
17	**step**	Stufe
20	**through** [θruː]	durch
21	**over**	über
21	**railway line** ['reɪlweɪ laɪn]	Eisenbahnlinie, Gleis
21	**up** [ʌp]	hinauf

24

Then you walk over the railway line. And then there are forty-nine steps down!"

"OK, then," says Carol. "Ninety-nine steps, here we come!"

5 3. The walk through the woods is great. The weather is nice, and the trees are all different colours – yellow, brown, and red. After an hour they come to the steps.

"Look, here are the steps. And that's the old railway line at the top," says Linda.

10 "Let's count the steps," says Lester. "One, two, three ..."
Whisky runs up. He is very fast. The friends go behind him. There are a lot of steps.

"Forty-eight, forty-nine, fifty!" says Lester. "Here we are at the top!"

15 "Here's the old railway line," says Kevin. "No trains go along here now, of course."

"You can see that," says Carol. "Look at all the grass on the line."

"Look over there!" says Linda. "Rabbits!"

20 Three little wild rabbits are running along the old railway line. When they hear the children, they run into the woods.

"Hey, where's Whisky?" Kevin says suddenly. They look round. But they can't see him.

"Whisky! Come here! Whisky!"

7	**after** ['ɑːftə]	nach
9	**at the top** [ət ðə'tɒp]	oben
10	**count** [kaʊnt]	zählen
15	**train** [treɪn]	Zug

But Whisky doesn't come.

"We must look for him," says Kevin.

Carol goes down the steps again. Lester goes down the steps on the other side. Kevin goes left, and walks along the railway line. Linda goes right.

"Whisky! Whisky! Come here!"

4. Linda is looking for Whisky in the trees next to the railway line. Suddenly she hears him.

"Woof! Woof!"

Yes, that's Whisky! But where is he?

"Whisky! Come here! Come to me, Whisky!"

But he doesn't come. Linda listens.

"Woof! Woof!"

The dog's bark is coming from the right. There is an old signal-box next to the railway line. Is Whisky behind the signal-box? Linda runs and looks.

5. "Come here! Whisky's over here!"

"That's Linda," says Kevin. He and Lester and Carol are together again now – next to the railway line. "But where is she?"

"Look, she's over there, next to that old signal-box," says Lester. They all run to the signal-box. Linda is waiting for them.

"Woof! Woof!"

4	**other** [ˈʌðə]	andere, -r, -s
4	**side** [saɪd]	Seite
14	**bark** [bɑːk]	Bellen
15	**signal-box** [ˈsɪgnəl bɒks]	Stellwerk

26

"That's Whisky!" says Kevin. "But where is he?"

"In the signal-box, I think," says Linda.

"What?" says Lester. "In the signal-box? But how – ?"

"Look," says Linda, "There's a big rabbit hole here."

5 They all look. Behind the signal-box there is a very big rabbit hole.

"And Whisky loves rabbits!" says Kevin. "When he sees a rabbit, he follows it, of course – "

"So Whisky sees a rabbit on the railway line," says
10 Linda. "Then it goes into this hole – "

"And Whisky follows it!" says Carol.

"But how does Whisky get into the signal-box?" says Lester.

"I think the rabbit hole goes under the signal-box," says
15 Linda. "I don't know!"

Kevin goes to the door, but he can't open it. And there is no key. "What can we do?" he says.

"Woof!" says Whisky. He can hear them, of course. But he can't come to them.

20 "What about the window?" says Carol.

"Oh yes! Maybe we can climb through the window!" says Lester.

6. The window is broken. Maybe they can open it from outside. But it is very high.

25 "How can we climb up?" says Linda.

4	**hole** [həʊl]	Loch
4	**rabbit hole**	Kaninchenbau
21	**climb** [klaɪm]	klettern
24	**high** [haɪ]	hoch

"You're small, Kevin," says Lester. "Maybe you can climb on my shoulders – "

"No, wait! there's a ladder next to the railway line over there! Look!"

5 It's a very old ladder, but it's long.

"Great! We can use that. I think it's OK," says Kevin. "Let's see."

They take the ladder and carry it to the signal-box. Then Kevin climbs up.

10 "Can you open the window?" asks Lester.

"Wait," answers Kevin. "I think I can. – Yes! I've got it open now! Good!"

He looks through the window into the signal-box. He can see Whisky now.

15 "Oh, Whisky! There you are! Are you OK? I'm coming, don't worry!"

Kevin climbs through the window. Inside the signal-box there is a high desk next to the window.

"The old signalman's desk!" Kevin thinks.

20 He goes down the steps to the door. And there is Whisky!

"Woof!" says Whisky. "Woof, woof!"

"Come with me, Whisky," says Kevin. "But wait – where's that rabbit hole? Show me, old boy!"

25 7. Then Kevin sees something. In the corner, there is a small cupboard. The little door is open. Kevin looks

2	**shoulder** [ˈʃəʊldə]	Schulter
3	**ladder** [ˈlædə]	Leiter
17	**inside** [ɪnˈsaɪd]	innerhalb, innen drin
18	**desk**	Pult
19	**signalman** [ˈsɪgnəlmən]	Stellwerkswärter
24	**show** [ʃəʊ]	zeigen

inside. At the back, there is a big hole. The rabbit hole! But inside the cupboard, there is a big black box. What is it?

"Hey, Carol! Linda! Lester! Come here! I must show you something!"

5 So the other three climb up the ladder, too. Then they come in through the window – and down the steps.

"Look here!" says Kevin. And he shows them the black box in the cupboard.

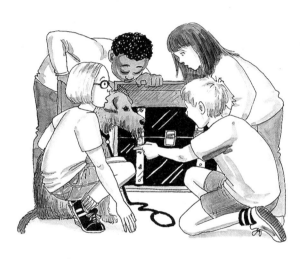

"What is it?" asks Linda. "It's very big!"

10 "Let's look inside," says Carol.

"Yes, let's open it!" says Lester.

1 **at the back** [ət ðəˈbæk]   hinten

But they can't open it. There is no key!

"Maybe there's treasure inside!" says Carol.

"Or money!" says Lester. "This is a robber's hidey-hole!"

"Let's take the box home!" says Linda.

But they can't carry the box. It is very, very heavy.

"We must go home and phone the police," says Kevin.
"Then they can come here and get the box."

"Great idea!" says Carol.

They help Whisky through the window. Then he jumps down.

"Hey, Whisky, are you OK?" says Linda.

"Woof!" says Whisky.

"He's OK!" says Kevin.

They all climb down the ladder. Then they carry it back to the railway line.

"Let's hope we don't meet the robbers on the ninety-nine steps!" says Carol.

"Robbers work at night – don't worry!" says Lester.

8. On Monday evening there is a phone call for Kevin. A policeman is on the telephone.

"Thank you for the tip about that hidey-hole," the policeman says. "Yes, we've got the black box now, Kevin. And yes, you and your friends are right! There's money inside. A lot of money! From a big bank robbery in

2	**treasure** [ˈtreʒə]	Schatz, Schätze
4	**hidey-hole** [ˈhaɪdɪhəʊl]	Versteck
5	**heavy** [ˈhevɪ].	schwer
16	**let's hope** [lets ˈhəʊp]	hoffen wir, hoffentlich
19	**phone call** [ˈfəʊnkɔːl]	Anruf
21	**tip**	Tipp, Hinweis
23	**you are right** [jʊəˈraɪt]	du hast Recht/ihr habt Recht!

September! – Listen, Kevin. Can you all come to the police station this week? Tuesday? Wednesday afternoon? We've got a nice reward for you all! Bye! And thank you again!"

"Do you hear that, Whisky?" says Kevin. "We're getting
5 a reward! And all because YOU like rabbits!"

17. How many rabbits?

TEACHER: This question is for you, Polly. Your dad gives you five rabbits. Then your grandpa gives you four rabbits. So – how many
10   rabbits have you got now?
POLLY: Ten.
TEACHER: Ten?
POLLY: Yes, ten. I've got one rabbit already.

---

1 **police station** [pə'li:s steɪʃən]   Polizeirevier, Präsidium
3 **reward** [rɪ'wɔ:d]   Belohnung
12 **already** [ɔ:l'redɪ].   schon

18. Susie's colour rhyme

What is green?
> *Fields and trees.*
Caterpillars, frogs –
> *And garden peas*.*

* * *

What is white?
> *Milk from the cow,*
The woods in winter –
> *It's snowing* now.*

* * *

What is blue?
> *The lake, the pool,*
The uniform
> *At Linda's school.*

* * *

What is red?
> *Jam – and cherries*,*
Traffic lights –
> *And summer berries*.*

* * *

pea / peas [piːz]   Erbse(n)
it's snowing ['snəʊɪŋ]   es schneit
cherry / cherries ['tʃerɪz]   Kirsche(n)
berry / berries ['berɪz]   Beere(n)

What is black?
> *A cat – a horse,*
An elephant
> *(At night, of course!)*

* * *

What is yellow?
> *Butter, cheese*,*
Ice cream, bananas –
> *Do you like these?*

* * *

What is brown?
> *A chocolate bar,*
A cup of coffee –
> *Here you are!*

* * *

Can you make pictures for the rhyme and put the colours in?

19. Sorry, Freddy!

Do you like the rhyme, Freddy?

Oh! Are you sleeping? Sorry, Freddy!

cheese [tʃiːz]   Käse

33

20. An animal puzzle*

animal   Tier
puzzle [ˈpʌzəl]   Rätsel

- ◆ You often find animals 10 → and 11 in the country. WOC HEESP PIPOH PLATHENE KEMNOY

- ◆ You can see animals 6, 8 and 13 at the zoo.

- ◆ You can ride on animal 4 → SHERO

- ◆ Animal 5 can fly – and it can talk! TROPRA

- ◆ Animal 7 sometimes helps the police. GOD

- ◆ Animals 4 ↓ and 10 ↓ and 12 are nice pets. STRAHME TAC TIBBAR

- ◆ Animal 2 can make a web. DIPSER

- ◆ Animal 3 can jump, and it likes water! GORF

- ◆ Animal 1 is an animal at home. EPT

- ◆ Animal 9 can walk, but it can't go very fast! RAPTILLECAR

21. Freddy, is that you?

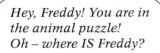

Hey, Freddy! You are in the animal puzzle! Oh – where IS Freddy?

Here I am, Susie. I can fly now, too! Look!

Oh, Freddy! Is that you?

Yes, it is, Susie. Freddy is a butterfly*, so I can't catch him now!

butterfly ['bʌtəflaɪ]   Schmetterling

Lösungen

Frogs: 1. green, yellow, brown / 2. jump, swim / 3. caterpillars, spiders / 4. sleep / 5. egg.

Elephants: 1. **16** / 2. **250** / 3. **150** / 4. **10** / 5. **4.**

Lesespaß im Abonnement

Let's start
Für Schülerinnen und Schüler
ab dem 1. Lernjahr
Klett-Nr. **97343**

A tot of English
Für Schülerinnen und
Schüler ab dem
2. Lernjahr
Klett-Nr. **97320**